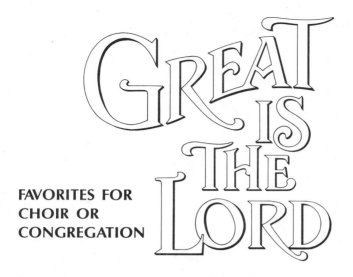

FAVORITES FOR CHOIR OR CONGREGATION

GREAT IS THE LORD

Arranged for use in Medleys or Individually
by Tom Fettke

Compiled by Ken Bible

D1403167

Lillenas Publishing Co.
KANSAS CITY, MO. 64141

2

*Majesty Medley

Arr. by Tom Fettke

HOW MAJESTIC: unis.; div. at "O Lord, we praise" (both times). HE IS LORD: unis. MAJESTY: div.; ladies only (3-pt) at "So exalt"; choir div. resumes at D.S.

How Majestic Is Your Name

M. W. S.
Based on Psalm 8:1, Isaiah 9:6

MICHAEL W. SMITH

He Is Lord

Unknown
Based on Philippians 2:11

Unknown

Majesty

J. W. H.

JACK W. HAYFORD

6

*Praise Medley

Arr. by Tom Fettke

WE HAVE COME: v.1, div. SOMETIMES ALLELUIA: 1st ref. & v.1, unis.; 2nd ref. & v.2, div.; 3rd ref. & coda, unis. LORD, WE PRAISE YOU: vv. 1 & 2, div.; v. 3, unis.; tag, div.

We Have Come into His House

B. B.

BRUCE BALLINGER

1. We have come in - to His house and gath - ered in His name to wor - ship Him._____ We have come in - to His house and gath - ered in His name to wor - ship Him.__
2. So for - get a - bout your - self and con - cen - trate on Him and wor - ship Him._____ So for - get a - bout your - self and con - cen - trate on Him and wor - ship Him.__
3. Let us lift up ho - ly hands and mag - ni - fy His name and wor - ship Him._____ Let us lift up ho - ly hands and mag - ni - fy His name and wor - ship Him.__

Song ending

Medley ending

Lord.
Lord.   Lord.
Lord.

Sometimes Alleluia

CHUCK GIRARD

C. G.

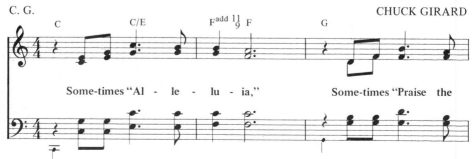

Some-times "Al - le - lu - ia,"   Some-times "Praise the

Lord, We Praise You

OTIS SKILLINGS

O. S.

© 1972 by Lillenas Publishing Co. All rights reserved.

*Exaltation Medley

Arr. by Tom Fettke

Use suggested intro. BE EXALTED: div. EL-SHADDAI: v.1, solo (opt.); v.2, ladies unis.; v.3, men unis.; D.S. v.1, unis. (or solo, then unis. on last phrase); THOU ART WORTHY: div.

Be Exalted, O God

Psalm 57:9-11
Adapted by B. C.

BRENT CHAMBERS

*El Shaddai

M. C. and J. T.

MICHAEL CARD and JOHN THOMPSON

*Translations of Hebrew terms:

El Shaddai—God Almighty; see Gen. 17:1
El Elyon—the Most High God; see Gen. 14:18-20
na Adonai—O Lord.
Erkahmka—we will love You.

14

praise and lift___ You high,___ El Shad - dai.___ 2. Thro' Your love
by Your might You set Your chil-dren free.___ 3. Thro' the years

stand; Your most awe-some work was done___ In the frail-ty of__ Your

Son. El Shad-dai, nai; I will praise You till__ I

die, El Shad-dai.___

Song ending | Medley ending

Thou Art Worthy

P. M. M.   PAULINE M. MILLS

Thou art wor - thy, Thou art wor - thy, Thou art

*Adoration Medley

Arr. by Tom Fettke

FATHER, I ADORE YOU: v.1, unis.; v.2, ladies unis.; v.3, 2-pt. round using 2 mixed groups (accompanist must repeat 1st 2 meas.).HOLY, HOLY: v.1, div.; v.2, ladies unis.; v.3, all div. GREAT IS THE LORD: 1st time, unis. then div. at double bar; 2nd time, ladies unis. on phrase 1, men unis. on phrase 2, all div. at double bar & on D.S.

Father, I Adore You
*Round

TERRYE COELHO

1. Fa - ther,
2. Je - sus, I a - dore You; (1) Lay my life be-
3. Spir - it,

fore You. How I love You!

love You! *same tempo*

★The accompaniment is optional. When the song is sung as a round, the accompaniment should probably be omitted.

© 1972 Maranatha! Music. All rights reserved. International copyright secured. Used by permission only.

*Arr. © 1984 by Pilot Point Music (ASCAP). All rights reserved.

Holy, Holy

J. O.

JIMMY OWENS

Song ending | CODA - Medley ending | New tempo ♩.= ca. 63

ho - ly.
Fa - ther.
Je - sus.   Je - sus.
Spir - it.
lu - jah.

Great Is the Lord

M. W. S. and D. D. S.   MICHAEL W. SMITH and DEBORAH D. SMITH

Great is the Lord, He is ho - ly and just; By His pow-er we trust in His love. _____ Great is the Lord, He is faith-ful and true; By His

20

*Glorify Him Medley

Arr. by Tom Fettke

MY TRIBUTE: unis.; div. at "To God. . ."; ladies unis. at "Just let"; all div. at "With His". BLESS HIS
HOLY NAME: div.; 1st "He has", men unis.; 2nd "He has", ladies unis.; 3rd "He has", all div. to end.
A PERFECT HEART: div., with medley ending.

My Tribute

A. C.

ANDRAÉ CROUCH

How____ can I say thanks for the things You have done for
me? Things____ so un-de-served, yet You gave____ to prove Your
love for me. The voic-es____ of a mil-lion an-gels____ could not ex-

Bless His Holy Name

A. C.

ANDRAÉ CROUCH

A Perfect Heart

D. M. and R. R.

DONY McGUIRE and REBA RAMBO

*Cornerstone Medley

Arr. by Tom Fettke

I GO: v.1, men unis.; both refs., all div.; v.2, ladies unis. CORNERSTONE: v.1, all unis.; v.2, div.; ladies unis. at "Rock of Ages"; 2nd "Rock of Ages", men unis.; "Till the breaking", all div., with tag.

I Go to the Rock

D. R.

DOTTIE RAMBO

Cornerstone

L. G.

LARI GOSS

1. Je - sus is _____ the Cor - ner - stone; Came for
am _____ by sin op - pressed, On the

sin - ners to a - tone. Tho' re - ject - ed by His
Stone _____ I am at rest. When the seeds _____ of truth are

own, _____ He be - came _____ the Cor - ner - stone; _____
sown, _____ He re - mains _____ the Cor - ner - stone; _____ Je - sus

is _____ the Cor - ner - stone. _____ 2. When I stone. _____

*Until Then Medley

Arr. by Tom Fettke

Use suggested intro., 'TIL THE STORM: v.1, div.; ref., unis. until "Hold me", then div. & on repeat. I'LL
FLY AWAY: v.1, div.; both refs., div.; v.2, ladies 2-pt (or duet). UNTIL THEN: begin with ref., div. (all
refs. div.); v.1, solo or choir unis.; v. 2, div. (or ladies duet).

'Till the Storm Passes By

M. L.

MOSIE LISTER

1. In the dark of the mid-night have I oft hid my
2. Man-y times Sa-tan whis-pered, "There is no need to
3. When the long night has end-ed and the storms come no

face, While the storm howls a-bove me, and there's
try, For there's no end of sor-row, there's no
more, Let me stand in Thy pres-ence on that

no hid-ing place. 'Mid the crash of the
hope by and by." But I know Thou art
bright, peace-ful shore. In that land where the

thun-der, pre-cious Lord, hear my cry; Keep me
with me, and to-mor-row I'll rise Where the
tem-pest nev-er comes, Lord, may I Dwell with

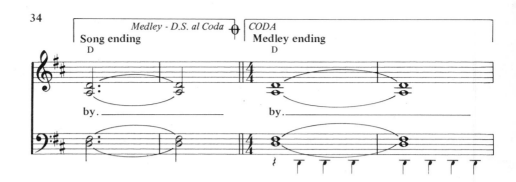

Medley - D.S. al Coda | CODA
Song ending | Medley ending

I'll Fly Away

A. E. B.

ALBERT E. BRUMLEY

1. Some glad morn-ing when this life is o'er, ____ I'll
2. When the shad-ows of this life have grown, ____ I'll
3. Just a few more wea-ry days and then ____ I'll fly a-way,

fly a - way.

fly a - way, fly a - way.

To a home on
Like a bird from
To a land where

fly a - way.

I'll fly a - way.

God's ce -les-tial shore, ____ I'll fly a-way, fly a - way, fly a-way.
pris - on bars has flown, ____ I'll fly a-way, fly a - way, fly a- way.
joys shall nev-er end, ____

fly a - way.

Until Then

S. H.

STUART HAMBLEN

1. My heart can sing when I pause to re- mem-ber A heart-ache here is but a step-ping stone A-long a trail that's wind-ing al-ways up-ward—

2. The things of earth will dim and lose their val-ue If we re-call they're bor-rowed for a-while; And things of earth that cause the heart to trem-ble,

3. This wea-ry world with all its toil and strug-gle May take its toll of mis-er-y and strife. The soul of man is like a wait-ing fal-con—

*Resurrection Medley

Arr. by Tom Fettke

Use suggested intro., RISE AGAIN: v.1, unis.; all refs., div.; v.2, solo or ladies unis.; v.3, all div. EASTER SONG: 1st 8 meas., unis.; div. on repeat and through rest of song. BECAUSE HE LIVES: ref., div.; v.1, men unis.; 2nd ref., div., to Coda.

Rise Again

D. H.

DALLAS HOLM

*Arr. © 1984 by Pilot Point Music (ASCAP). All rights reserved.

Easter Song

A. H.

ANNE HERRING

1. Hear the bells ring - ing, they're sing - ing that
2. Hear the bells ring - ing, they're sing - ing "Christ

we can be born a - gain!
is ris - en from the dead!"

The an - gel up - on the tomb - stone said, "He is ris - en just as He said.

Because He Lives

W. J. and GLORIA GAITHER

WILLIAM J. GAITHER

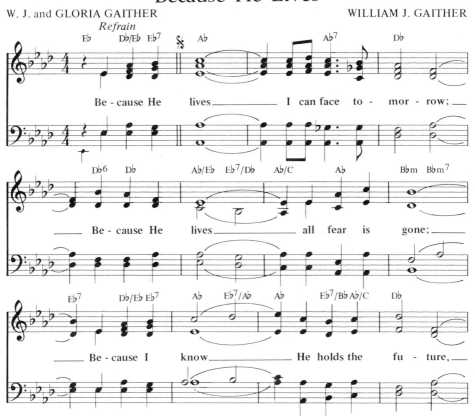

44

*Testimony Medley

Arr. by Tom Fettke

Use suggested intro., HE TOUCHED ME: v.1, sop.-ten. duet or choir div.; ref., choir div. to medley ending.
SOMETHING BEAUTIFUL: ladies unis. I WILL SERVE THEE: vv. 1 & 2, men unis.; ref., choir div. THE
LONGER I SERVE HIM: div.

He Touched Me

W. J. G.

WILLIAM J. GAITHER

Something Beautiful

GLORIA GAITHER

WILLIAM J. GAITHER

Some-thing beau-ti-ful, some-thing good;
All my con-fu-sion He un-der-stood.
All I had to of-fer Him was bro-ken-ness and
strife, But He made some-thing beau-ti-ful of my

Song ending life. **Medley ending** life.

I Will Serve Thee

W. J. G.

WILLIAM J. GAITHER

lives   are   why   You   died   on   Cal - v'ry.

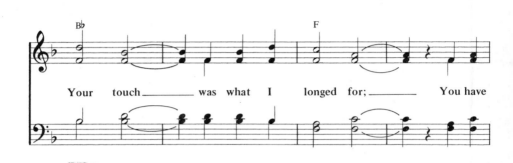

Your   touch_____ was   what   I   longed   for;_____ You have

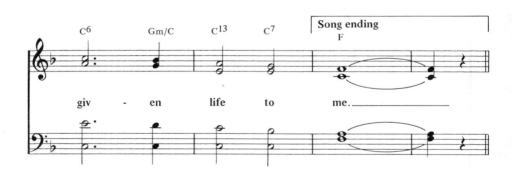

giv - en   life   to   me._____

me._____

The Longer I Serve Him

W. J. G.

WILLIAM J. GAITHER

1. Since I start - ed for the King - dom,
2. Ev - 'ry need He is sup - ply - ing,

Since my life He con - trols,_____
Plen - teous grace He be - stows._____

Since I gave my heart to Je - sus, The
Ev - 'ry day my way gets bright - er; The

long - er I serve____ Him, the sweet - er He grows.
long - er I serve____ Him, the sweet - er He grows. The

52

*Joy Medley

Arr. by Tom Fettke

THE JOY: v.1, unis.; v.2, men unis.; v.3, ladies unis. THE TREES: unis. (opt.—on repeat of ref., men and women alternate on "The trees of the field will clap their hands"; all on "while you go out").

The Joy of the Lord

A. G. V.   ALLIENE G. VALE

1. The joy_____ of the Lord_____ is my
2. He gives me liv - ing wa - ter and I thirst no
3. The word of faith is nigh thee, e - ven in thy

54

CODA - Medley ending

strength._____

The Trees of the Field

STEFFI GEISER RUBIN
Based on Isaiah 55:12

STUART DAUERMANN

You shall go out with joy___ and be led forth with peace; _____ The moun-tains

and the hills will break forth be - fore you. There'll be

The trees of the field will clap their hands _____ While you go out with joy. joy. joy. And shout when we go out with joy.

(Trax: add 4 beats to hold on "joy")

*Trust Medley

Arr. by Tom Fettke

Use suggested intro., THROUGH IT ALL: v.1, unis.; both refs., div.; v.2, solo or unis. ladies. PEACE IN THE MIDST: choir div. LEARNING TO LEAN: all refs., div.; v.1, solo; 2nd ref., take D.S.

Through It All

A. C.

ANDRAÉ CROUCH

I've had man-y   tears   and sor-rows;   I've had ques-tions
I ___ thank God   for   the moun-tains   And I thank Him

for   to-mor-row;   There've been times I   did-n't know right from
for   the val-leys;   I thank Him for   the   storms_ He brought me

wrong. _____   But in   ev-'ry sit-u-
through; _____   For if   I'd nev-er

60

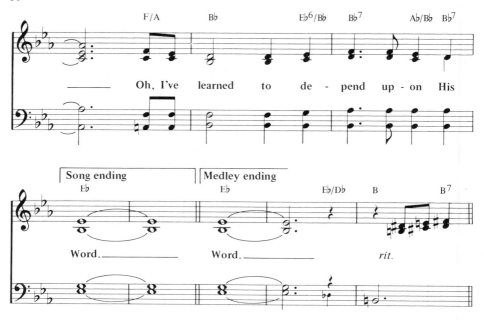

Oh, I've learned to de-pend up-on His

Song ending | Medley ending

Word. | Word. | *rit.*

Peace in the Midst of the Storm

S. R. A.

STEPHEN R. ADAMS

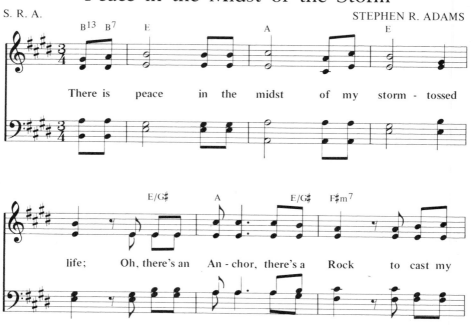

There is peace in the midst of my storm - tossed

life; Oh, there's an An - chor, there's a Rock to cast my

Learning to Lean

J. S.

JOHN STALLINGS

1. A joy I can't ex - plain _____ is fill - ing my soul
2. There's glo - ri - ous vic - t'ry each day now for me

Since the day I met Je - sus, my King. _____
As I dwell in His peace so se - rene. _____

His bless - ed Ho - ly Spir - it is lead - ing my way;
He helps me with each task _____ if on - ly I ask;

He is teach - ing, and I'm learn - ing to lean. _____
Ev - 'ry day now I am learn - ing to lean. _____

D.C. al fine

*Christlike Medley

Arr. by Tom Fettke

HE'S STILL WORKIN': div. on all refs.; v.1, ladies unis.; v.2, men unis. LET THE BEAUTY: choir unis.
2 CORINTHIANS 3:18: 1st time, div.; 2nd time, unis., then div. from "The love of God shown" to end;
take tag ending.

He's Still Workin' on Me

J. H.

JOEL HEMPHILL

Let the Beauty of Jesus Be Seen in Me

ALBERT W. T. ORSBORN

TOM JONES

2 Corinthians 3:18

Adapted

Unknown

From glo - ry to glo - ry He's chang - ing me,

Chang - ing me, chang - ing me; His

like - ness and im - age to per - fect in me— The

love of God shown to the world._____ For He's

68

*Second Coming Medley

Arr. by Tom Fettke

COMING AGAIN: v.1, div.; v.2, ladies unis.; v.3, men unis.; v.4, choir div. REDEMPTION DRAWETH NIGH: v.1 & both refs., div.; v.2, solo or choir unis. WE SHALL BEHOLD HIM: v.1, solo; both refs., div.; v.2, solo (choir "oo", no sop.); medley ending.

Coming Again

M. L.

MOSIE LISTER

1. Je - sus is com - ing; Je - sus is
2. In clouds of glo - ry, Bright clouds of
3. We'll rise to meet ___ Him, Rise up to
4. We shall be like ___ Him; We shall be
5. Oh, hal - le - lu - jah! Oh, hal - le -

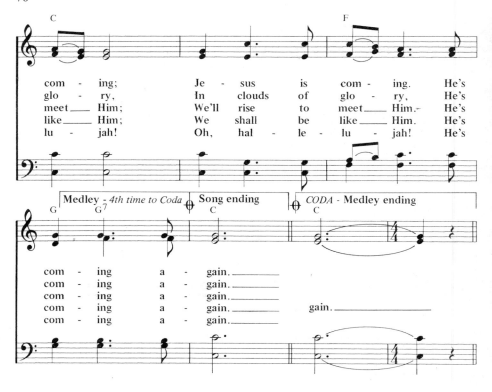

com - ing;	Je - sus is	com - ing.	He's
glo - ry,	In clouds of	glo - ry,	He's
meet___ Him;	We'll rise to	meet___ Him.-	He's
like___ Him;	We shall be	like ___ Him.	He's
lu - jah!	Oh, hal - le - lu -	jah!	He's

Medley - *4th time to Coda* | **Song ending** | **CODA** - **Medley ending**

com - ing a - gain.___	
com - ing a - gain.___	
com - ing a - gain.___	
com - ing a - gain.___	gain.___
com - ing a - gain.___	

Redemption Draweth Nigh

G. J.   GORDON JENSEN

1. Years of time have come and gone since I
2. Wars and strife on ev - 'ry hand, and___

first___ heard it told, How Je - sus would
vio - lence fills our land; Still some peo - ple

72

We Shall Behold Him

D. R.

DOTTIE RAMBO

*Wait Medley

Arr. by Tom Fettke

Use suggested intro., IN HIS TIME: v.1, unis. WE MUST WAIT: v.1, solo or unis.; v.2, ladies unis., men sing echo. THEY THAT WAIT: div.; use D.S. as tag.

In His Time

D. B.

DIANE BALL

© 1978 Maranatha! Music. All rights reserved. International copyright secured. Used by permission only.

*Arr. © 1984 by Pilot Point Music (ASCAP). All rights reserved.

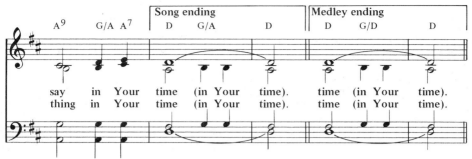

We Must Wait

RANDY THOMAS

learn my les-sons well. In His tim-ing He will
learn our les-sons well. In His tim-ing He will
learn your les-sons well. In His tim-ing He will

Medley - 2nd time to Coda

tell__ me what to do,_____ where to go,_____ what to say..
tell__ us what to do,_____ where to go,_____ what to say..
tell__ you what to do,_____ where to go,_____ what to say..

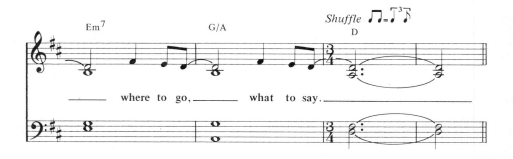

Song ending

CODA - Medley ending

What to do,_

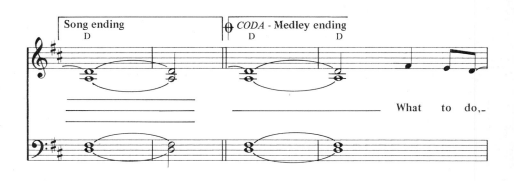

where to go,_____ what to say._____

Shuffle

They That Wait upon the Lord

S. H.

STUART HAMBLEN

*Saved Medley

Arr. by Tom Fettke

Use suggested intro., THEN I MET: v.1, unis.; both refs., div.; v.2, solo or unis. I'VE BEEN CHANGED:
v.1, ladies unis.; all refs., div.; v.2, men unis.; v.4, div.

Then I Met the Master

M. L.

MOSIE LISTER

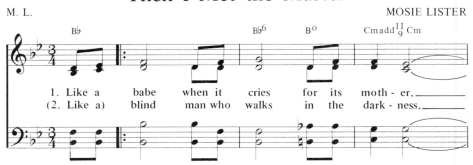

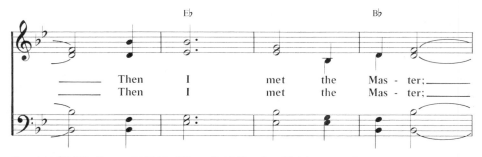

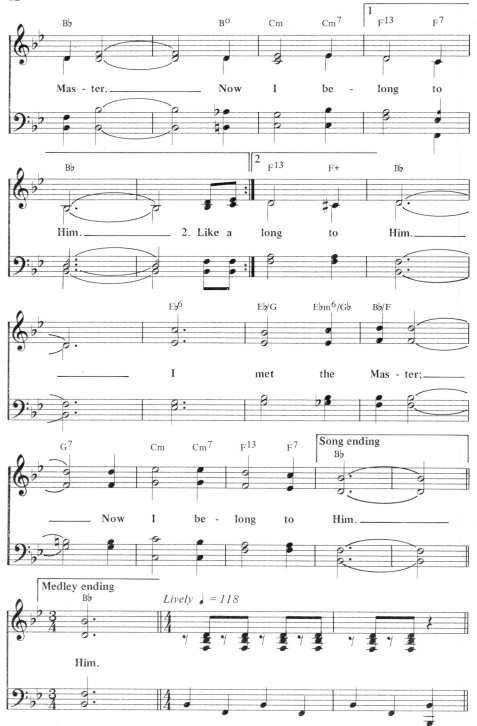

I've Been Changed

M. L.

MOSIE LISTER

1. Well, I've been to the riv - er, I've been bap - tized; I've been
2. Though my sins were as scar - let, they're white as snow. I was
3. Like the poor He - brew chil - dren I wan - dered long In a
4. When at last in His pres-ence I stand a - bove, He will

washed in the blood of the Lamb. I've been changed from the
bound but to - day I am free. I was lost in the
bare des - ert land to and fro; But I crossed o - ver
wipe all the tears from my eyes; And I'll thank Him for

crea - ture that once I was, And Re - deemed is now my
dark - ness but now am found. I was blind but now I
Jor - dan to Ca - naan's land, Where the milk and hon - ey
giv - ing a wretch like me Last - ing hope be - yond the

name. I've been changed, I've been new-born; _____ All my
see. I've been changed, I'm new - born now; My
flow.
skies.

*Shepherd Medley

Arr. by Tom Fettke

THE NEW 23RD: div.; ladies unison at "Guarding, guiding"; div. at "With blessing". GENTLE SHEPHERD:
vv. 1 & 2, sop.-alto-ten. only (or trio); all div. at "There's no other"; v.3, div.

The New 23rd

R. C.

RALPH CARMICHAEL

Gentle Shepherd

W. J. and GLORIA GAITHER

WILLIAM J. GAITHER

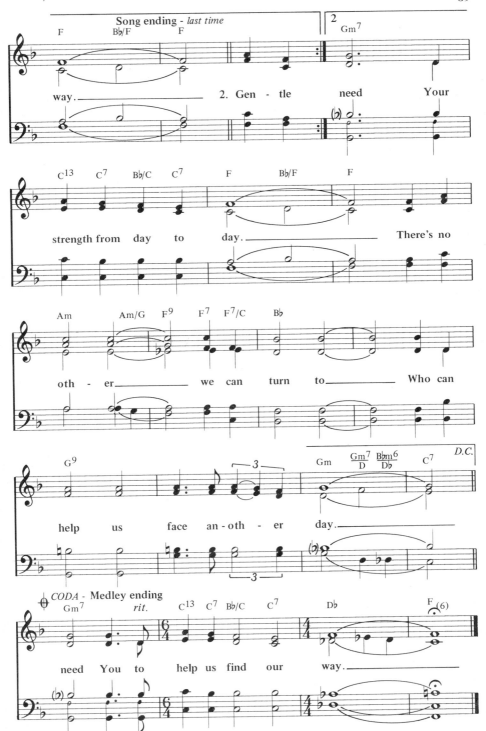

*Reach Out Medley

Arr. by Tom Fettke

Use suggested intro., LET ME TOUCH HIM: v.1 & ref., div. REACH OUT TO JESUS: v.1 & both refs., div.; v.2, men unis.; tag ending.

Let Me Touch Him

V. E.

VEP ELLIS

1. Let me touch Him, let me touch Je-sus; Let me touch Him as He pass-es by. Then when I shall reach out to oth-ers, They shall know Him, they shall live and not die.

2. I was stray-ing so far from Je-sus; I was lone-ly, had no peace with-in. Then the hand of my Sav-ior touched me; Now I'm reach-ing to oth-ers in sin.

3. There's a riv-er, a riv-er flow-ing From with-in and to cleanse my soul; And the flow sets my life to glow-ing— Ho-ly Spir-it, more than sil-ver and gold.

Chorus

A G/A F#m/A A7 D

Oh, to be His hand ex-tend-ed,_____ Reach-ing

A G/A F#m/A A9 D *Suggested introduction* G

out to the op-press'd!_____ Let me touch Him, let

D G/B Gm6/Bb D/A

me touch Je-sus_____ So that oth-ers may

A7 G/A A7 | Song ending | Medley ending
D | D D7

know and be blessed._____ blessed._____

Reach Out to Jesus

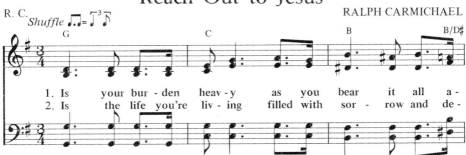

R. C. *Shuffle* ♩.♪ = ♪³♪

RALPH CARMICHAEL

G   C   B   B/D#

1. Is   your bur-den heav-y   as you   bear   it all a-
2. Is   the life you're liv-ing filled with sor-row and de-

*Holy Spirit Medley

Arr. by Tom Fettke

SPIRIT OF THE LIVING GOD: div. HOLY SPIRIT, THOU ART WELCOME: 1st ref., ladies (with cued notes); v.1, choir unis.; 2nd ref. and v.2, div. WHERE THE SPIRIT: section 1, men unis.; section 2, choir div.; take repeat.

Spirit of the Living God

D. I.

DANIEL IVERSON

Holy Spirit, Thou Art Welcome

D. R. and D. H.

DOTTIE RAMBO and
DAVID HUNTSINGER

wel - come in____ this place.____ 1. Lord, in Thy
2. Fill all the

pres-ence there's heal - ing di - vine;____ No oth - er
hun - gry and emp - ty with - in. Re - store us, oh,

pow - er can save, Lord, but Thine. Ho - ly Spir-it, Thou art
Fa - ther; re - vive us a - gain.

wel - come in this place, Thou art wel - come

in____ this place.____ place.____

Song ending
Music ending

Where the Spirit of the Lord Is

S. R. A.

STEPHEN R. ADAMS

*Rejoice Medley

Arr. by Tom Fettke

Use suggested intro., I WILL SING: div.; 2-pt ladies at "With my mouth"; div. again at "I will sing". THIS
IS THE DAY: 1st time, unis. (opt.-use select echo choir on bracketed portions); 2nd time, div. (opt.-with
echo quartet). COME INTO HIS PRESENCE: 4-pt round, a cappella.

I Will Sing of the Mercies

Adapted from Psalm 89:1

Unknown
Arr. by David Cole and Tom Fettke

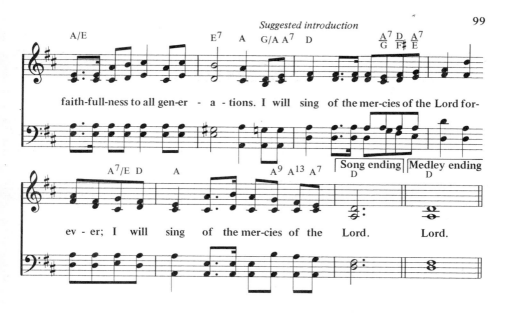

Suggested introduction

faith-full-ness to all gen-er - a -tions. I will sing of the mer-cies of the Lord for-

ev - er; I will sing of the mer-cies of the Lord. Lord.

Song ending | Medley ending

This Is the Day

L. G.

LES GARRETT
Arr. by Tom Fettke

This is the day, this is the day that the Lord has made,

Echo

that the Lord has made. We will re -joice,

we will re -joice and be glad in it, and be

*2nd time—Segue to "Come Into His Presence" (a cappella—orchestral track ends here.)

Come into His Presence
Round

Unknown   Unknown

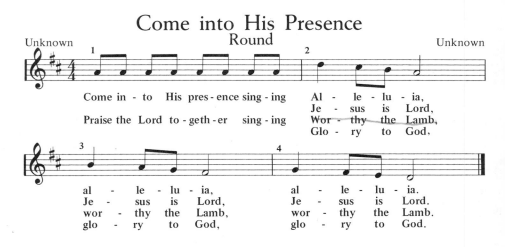

Come in - to His pres - ence sing - ing Al - le - lu - ia,
Praise the Lord to - geth - er sing - ing Wor - thy the Lamb,
Glo - ry to God,

al - le - lu - ia,   al - le - lu - ia.
Je - sus is Lord,   Je - sus is Lord.
wor - thy the Lamb,   wor - thy the Lamb.
glo - ry to God,   glo - ry to God.

*His Care Medley

Arr. by Tom Fettke

Use suggested intro., HIS EYE: v.1, unis.; ref., div.; to medley ending. HE CARES: v.1, unis. or solo; both refs., div.; v.2, ladies unis. THE WONDER: v.1 & ref. with D.S., div.

His Eye Is on the Sparrow

Mrs. C. D. MARTIN   CHARLES H. GABRIEL

1. Why should I feel dis - cour-aged,_____ Why should the shad - ows
2. "Let not your heart be trou-bled,"_____ His ten - der word I
3. When-ev - er I am temp-ted,_____ When-ev - er clouds a -

come,_____ Why should my heart be lone - ly_____
hear;_____ And rest - ing on His good-ness_____
rise,_____ When songs give place to sigh - ing,_____

And long for heav'n and home_____ When Je - sus is_____ my
I lose my doubt and fears._____ Tho' by the path_____ He
When hope with-in me dies,_____ I draw the clos - er

103

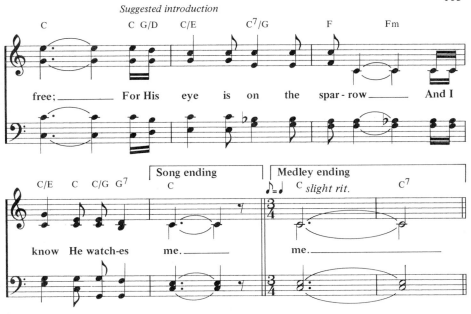

free;_____ For His eye is on the spar-row_____ And I

know He watch-es me._____ me._____

Song ending

Medley ending *slight rit.*

He Cares for Me

J. O.

JIMMY OWENS

1. Our God is far great-er than____ words can make
2. The earth and the heav-ens are the work of His
3. He rides the wild heav-ens, He____ strides thro' the

known. Ex - alt - ed and ho - ly, He
hands, And bil - lions of an - gels o -
seas; The high moun-tains trem - ble to

© 1971 by Lillenas Publishing Co. All rights reserved.

The Wonder of It All

G. B. S.

GEORGE BEVERLY SHEA

*God's Love Medley

Arr. by Tom Fettke

Use suggested intro., IF THAT ISN'T LOVE: v.1, unis.; ref., div. OH HOW HE LOVES: div. THE LOVE OF GOD: v.1, ladies unis.; both refs., div.; v.3, sop. or ten. solo, alto-ten.-bass "oo" parts; use opt. tag.

If That Isn't Love

D. R.

DOTTIE RAMBO

1. He left the splen-dor of heav-en, _____ Know-ing His
2. E - ven in death He re - mem-bered _____ The thief hang - ing

des - ti - ny _____ Was the lone - ly
by _____ His side. _____ He spoke with

hill of Gol - goth - a; _____ There to lay down His
love and com - pas - sion; _____ Then He took him to

Refrain

life _____ for me. _____ If that is - n't love _____
Par - a - dise. _____

Oh, How He Loves You and Me

K. K.

KURT KAISER

The Love of God

F. M. L.

F. M. LEHMAN
Arr. by Claudia Lehman May

1. The love of God is great-er far——Than tongue or pen can ev - er tell;
2. When years of time shall pass a - way,——And earth-ly thrones and kingdoms fall,
3. Could we with ink the o - cean fill,——And were the skies of parchment made,

It goes be - yond the high-est star,——And reach-es to the low-est hell.
When men, who here re-fuse to pray,——On rocks and hills and mountains call,
Were ev-'ry stalk on earth a quill,——And ev - 'ry man a scribe by trade,

The guilt-y pair, bowed down with care,——God gave His Son—— to win;
God's love so sure shall still en - dure,——All meas-ure-less—— and strong;
To write the love of God a - bove Would drain the o - cean dry.

*Consecration Medley

Arr. by Tom Fettke

Use suggested intro., LORD, BE GLORIFIED: v.1, unis.; v.2, div. MY DESIRE: 2-pt ladies or duet. TO
BE USED: choir div. THE GREATEST THING: v.1, unis.; v.2, solo; v.3, div.

Lord, Be Glorified

B. K.

BOB KILPATRICK

My Desire

L. P.

LILLIAN PLANKENHORN

My de-sire—— to be like Je-sus; My de-sire—— to be like Him!—— His Spir-it fill me,—— His love o'er-whelm me;—— In deed and word—— to be like Him!—— Him! ——

Song ending
C

Medley ending
C *faster*

To Be Used of God

A. M.

AUDREY MEIER

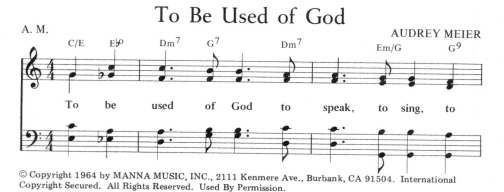

To be used of God to speak, to sing, to

The Greatest Thing

M. P.

MARK PENDERGRASS

The great-est thing____ in all my life is {know-ing / lov-ing / serv-ing} You.____ The great-est thing____ in all my life is {know-ing / lov-ing / serv-ing} You.____ I want to {know / love / serve} You more; I want to {know / love / serve} You more. The great-est thing____ in all my life is {know-ing / lov-ing / serv-ing} You.

*The Bond of Love Medley

Arr. by Tom Fettke

Use suggested intro., I AM LOVED: div. THE BOND OF LOVE: v.1 and ref., unis.; v.2 and ref., div.
THE FAMILY OF GOD: unis.

I Am Loved

W. J. and GLORIA GAITHER

WILLIAM J. GAITHER

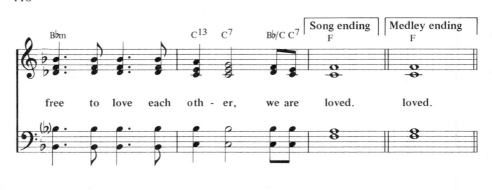

free   to   love   each   oth - er,   we are   loved.   loved.

The Bond of Love

O. S.

OTIS SKILLINGS

1. Love through Christ has   brought us to-geth - er,   Melt - ing our hearts as
2. Now, dear Lord, we   join   in__ wor - ship;   Thank You for all You've

one.   By   God's   Spir - it   we   are u - nit - ed,
done.   Thank You   for   this   love   You __ gave __ us;

One through His bless - ed   Son.
Thank You for mak-ing us   one.   We are   one in the bond of

The Family of God

W.J.G. and GLORIA GAITHER

WILLIAM J. GAITHER

120

*Cross Medley

Arr. by Tom Fettke

Use suggested intro., HE LOOKED BEYOND: unis.; div. at "I shall forever". I WILL GLORY: v.1, solo;
1st ref., choir div.; v.2 & ref., div.

He Looked Beyond My Fault

DOTTIE RAMBO   Adapted from "Londonderry Aire"

I Will Glory in the Cross

D. R.

DOTTIE RAMBO

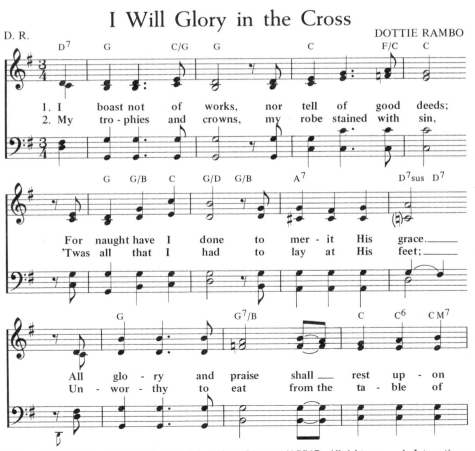

1. I boast not of works, nor tell of good deeds;
2. My tro-phies and crowns, my robe stained with sin,

For naught have I done to mer-it His grace.
'Twas all that I had to lay at His feet;

All glo-ry and praise shall ___ rest up - on
Un - wor - thy to eat from the ta - ble of

*Pass It On Medley

Arr. by Tom Fettke

Use suggested intro., PASS IT ON: v.1, ladies unis.; all refs., choir div.; v.3, unis. or solo. I'LL TELL THE
WORLD: v.1, div. LORD, LAY SOME SOUL: div.

Pass It On

K. K.

KURT KAISER

1. It ____ on - ly takes a spark to get a fire ____ go - ing, ____ And soon all those a - round can warm up in its glow - ing. ____ That's
2. What a won - drous time is spring when all the trees are bud - ding, ____ The birds be - gin to sing, the flow - ers start their bloom - ing. ____ That's
3. I ____ wish for you, my friends, this hap - pi - ness that I've found; ____ pass it on! You can de - pend on Him, It mat - ters not where you're bound. ____ pass it on! I'll

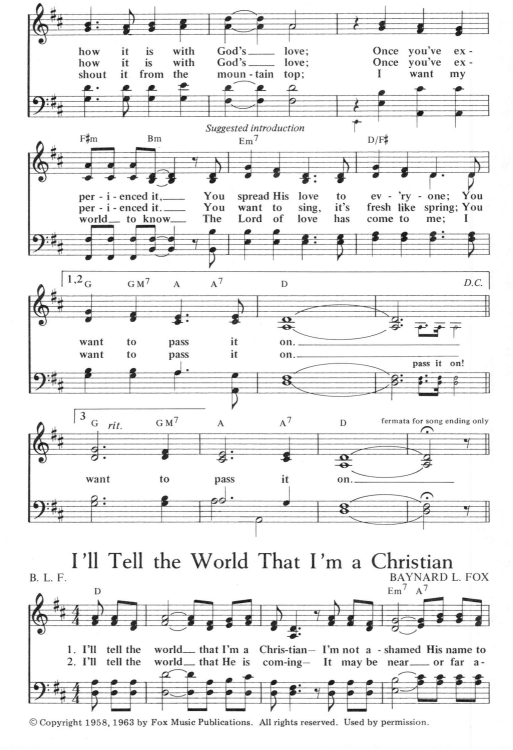

how it is with God's ___ love; Once you've ex-
how it is with God's ___ love; Once you've ex-
shout it from the moun-tain top; I want my

Suggested introduction

per - i - enced it, ___ You spread His love to ev - 'ry - one; You
per - i - enced it, ___ You want to sing, it's fresh like spring; You
world ___ to know ___ The Lord of love has come to me; I

1,2
want to pass it on. ___
want to pass it on. ___
pass it on!

3 *rit.*
want to pass it on. ___
fermata for song ending only

I'll Tell the World That I'm a Christian

B. L. F.   BAYNARD L. FOX

1. I'll tell the world ___ that I'm a Chris-tian— I'm not a-shamed His name to
2. I'll tell the world ___ that He is com-ing— It may be near ___ or far a-

one____ could love me so; My life, my all____ is His for-
shamed_ His name to bear; O tell the world____that you're a

Song ending **Medley ending**

ev - er, And where He leads me I will go. go.
Chris-tian, And take Him with you ev-'ry-where.__

Lord, Lay Some Soul upon My Heart

Dr. LEON TUCKER   IRA D. SANKEY

Lord, lay some soul up - on my heart, And

love that soul through me;_____ And may I glad - ly

do my part To win that soul for Thee.____

*God's Grace Medley

Arr. by Tom Fettke

Use suggested intro., GOD'S GREAT GRACE: v.1, ladies unis.; both refs., choir div.; v.3, unis. HIS GRACE
IS SUFFICIENT: v.1 and 1st ref., men unis.; v.2 & 2nd ref., choir div.

God's Great Grace

F. W. H.

FLOYD W. HAWKINS

1. The wis-dom of this world is so a-maz-ing, As
2. No man hath known, nor can we grasp by rea-son The
3. When pres-sures of this life in-crease the bur-den, When

men sur-vey the earth and dis-tant space; But there's a realm that's
reach of grace that lift-ed you and me. When we were sin-ners,
strength is need-ed in a-bun-dant store, 'Tis then we hear the

far be-yond all meas-ure—___ The fath-om-less ex-panse of God's great
still the Fa-ther loved us;___ 'Twas love that led my Lord to Cal-va-
Sav-ior's bless-ed prom-ise,___ "My grace is all-suf-fi-cient—trust Me

130

CODA - Medley ending

roll.　　accel.

His Grace Is Sufficient for Me

M. L.　　　　　　　　　　　　　　　　　　　　　　　　MOSIE LISTER

1. Man-y times I'm tried and test-ed as I trav-el day by day; Oft I meet with pain and sor-row, and there's trou-ble in the way. But I have the sweet as-sur-ance that my soul the Lord will lead, And in

2. When the temp-ter brings con-fu-sion and I don't know what to do, On my knees I turn to Je-sus, for I know He'll see me through. Then de-spair is changed to vic-t'ry, ev-'ry doubt just melts a-way, And in

*His Sacrifice Medley

Arr. by Tom Fettke

Use suggested intro., HE BECAME POOR: v.1 & both refs., div.; v.4, unis. TEN THOUSAND ANGELS: v.1, mixed quartet; all refs., choir div.; v.2, solo or unis. choir; v.3, unis. Great ritard at end of last refrain.

He Became Poor

B. C.

BYRON CARMONY

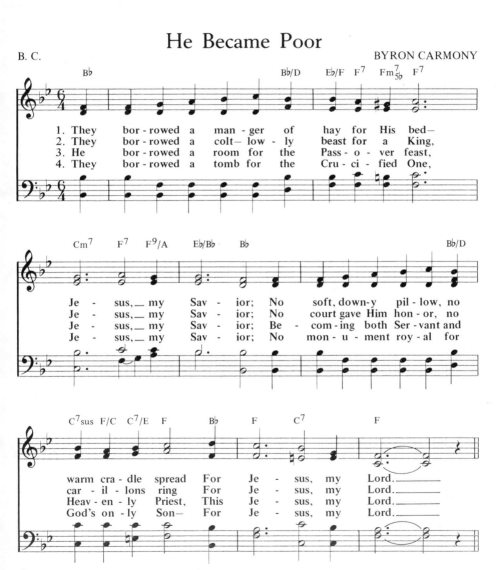

1. They bor-rowed a man-ger of hay for His bed—
2. They bor-rowed a colt— low-ly beast for a King,
3. He bor-rowed a room for the Pass-o-ver feast,
4. They bor-rowed a tomb for the Cru-ci-fied One,

Je - sus,__ my Sav - ior; No soft, down-y pil-low, no
Je - sus,__ my Sav - ior; No court gave Him hon-or, no
Je - sus,__ my Sav - ior; Be - com-ing both Ser-vant and
Je - sus,__ my Sav - ior; No mon-u-ment roy-al for

warm cra-dle spread For Je - sus, my Lord._____
car - il-lons ring For Je - sus, my Lord._____
Heav-en-ly Priest, This Je - sus, my Lord._____
God's on-ly Son— For Je - sus, my Lord._____

134

Ten Thousand Angels

R. O.

RAY OVERHOLT

1. They___ bound the hands of Je-sus in the gar-den where He prayed; They led Him thro' the streets in shame.___
2. Up-on His pre-cious head___ they___ placed a crown of thorns; They laughed and said, "Be-hold the King."___
3. Then they nailed Him to the Cross,___ His___ moth-er stood near-by; He said, "Wom-an, be-hold thy son!"___
4. To the howl-ing mob He yield-ed; He did not for mer-cy cry. The cross of shame He took a-lone.___

They spat up-on the Sav-ior, so___ pure and free from sin. They said, "Cru-ci-fy Him; He's to blame."___
They struck Him and they cursed Him and___ mocked His ho-ly name. All a-lone He suf-fered ev-'ry-thing.___
He cried, "I thirst for wa-ter," but they gave Him none to drink. Then the sin-ful work of man was done.___
And when He cried, "It's fin-ished," He ___ gave Him-self to die; Sal-va-tion's won-drous work was done.___

*Seek Ye First Medley

Arr. by Tom Fettke

Use suggested intro., SEEK YE FIRST: v.1, unis. ONLY ONE LIFE: v.1, sop.-alto-ten. trio; both refs., choir div.; v.3, solo or unis. WITH ETERNITY'S VALUES: div.

Seek Ye First

K. L.

KAREN LAFFERTY

1. Seek ye first the king - dom of God
2. Where two or three are gath - ered in my name,

And His righ - teous - ness; And all these
There am I in their midst; And what-so-

things shall be add - ed un - to you. Hal - le -
ev - er ye shall ask, I will do. Hal - le -

lu, hal - le - lu - jah.
lu, hal - le - lu - jah. jah.

Only One Life

L. W.

LANNY WOLFE

1. It_____ mat-ters so lit-tle how much you may
2. You may take all the trea-sures from far - a - way
3. The_____ days pass so swift-ly, the months come and

own, The plac - es you've been_____ or the peo - ple you've
lands,_____ Take all the rich - es you can hold in your
go, The years melt a - way_____ like_____ new fal - len

known. For it all comes to noth-ing when placed at His
hands, And_____ take all the plea-sures your mon - ey can
snow._____ Spring turns to sum-mer and sum - mer to

feet; It's noth - ing to Je - sus, just_____ mem -'ries to
buy; But what will you have_____ when it's your time to
fall; _____ Au - tumn brings win-ter, then_____ death comes to

With Eternity's Values in View

A. S.

AL SMITH

*Faith Medley

Arr. by Tom Fettke

Use suggested intro., GOT ANY RIVERS?: div. FAITH IN GOD: Sop.—alto-ten. trio, or choir div. GOD SAID IT: ref., ladies unis.; v.1, choir div.; repeat ref., unis.

Got Any Rivers?

O. E.

OSCAR ELIASON

Got an-y riv-ers you think are un-cross-a-ble?

Got an-y moun-tains you can't tun-nel thro'?

God spe-cial-iz-es in things thought im-pos-si-ble—

Suggested introduction **Medley** - *segue to "Faith in God"*

He does the things oth-ers can-not do.

Faith in God Can Move a Mountain

J. W. P. and A. B. S.

JOHN W. PETERSON and ALFRED B. SMITH

God Said It, I Believe It, That Settles It

S. R. A. and GENE BRAUN

STEPHEN R. ADAMS

God said it and I be-lieve it, And that set-tles it for me! God said it and I be-lieve it, And that set-tles it for me! Though some may doubt that His Word is true, I've cho-sen to be-lieve it; now how a-bout you? God

*Christot Within Medley

Arr. by Tom Fettke

Use suggested intro., I LIVE BY FAITH: men unis. GREATER IS HE: all refs., choir div.; v.1, solo; v.2, mixed quartet or choir unis.

I Live By Faith

Adapted from Galatians 2:20

C. C. DUNBAR

Greater Is He That Is in Me

L. W.

LANNY WOLFE

*Invitation Medley

Arr. by Tom Fettke

Use suggested intro., INTO MY HEART: solo or unis. HOW LONG: v.1, div.; v.2, ladies unis.; choir div. at "How long . . . since you woke"; use D.S. al fine.

Right Now

O. S.

OTIS SKILLINGS

Into My Heart

H. D. C.

HARRY D. CLARK

How Long Has It Been?

M.L.

MOSIE LISTER

1. How long has it been since you talked with the Lord, And told Him your heart's hid-den se-crets?_____ How long since you prayed, how long since you stayed On your knees 'til the light shone through?_____ How

2. How long has it been since you knelt by your bed And prayed to the Lord up in heav-en?_____ How long since you knew that He'd an-swer you And would keep you the long night through?_____ How

long has it been since your mind felt at ease? How
long has it been since you woke with the dawn And

long since your heart knew no bur - den?_____
felt that the day's worth the liv - ing?_____

Can you call Him your Friend?__ How long has it been since you

Medley - *D.S. al Fine (last verse)*

Fine

knew that He cares for you?_____

SONG INDEX

*A Perfect Heart 25

*Be Exalted, O God 11
*Because He Lives 43
*Bless His Holy Name 24

*Come Into His Presence 100
*Coming Again 69
*2 Corinthians 3:18 67
*Cornerstone 29

*Easter Song 41
*El-Shaddai 13

Faith in God Can Move a Mountain 142
*Father, I Adore You 16

*Gentle Shepherd 88
God Said It, I Believe It, That Settles It . 143
God's Great Grace 129
Got Any Rivers? 141
*Great Is the Lord 18
Greater Is He That Is in Me 146

He Became Poor 133
*He Cares for Me 103
*He Is Lord 4
He Looked Beyond My Fault 121
*He Touched Me 46
*He's Still Workin' on Me 64
*His Eye Is on the Sparrow 101
His Grace Is Sufficient for Me 131
*Holy, Holy 17
*Holy Spirit, Thou Art Welcome 95
How Long Has It Been? 150
*How Majestic Is Your Name 2

I Am Loved 117
*I Go to the Rock 26
I Live by Faith 145
I Will Glory in the Cross 123
*I Will Serve Thee 49
*I Will Sing of the Mercies 98
*I'll Fly Away 34
I'll Tell the World That I'm a Christian . . 126
*I've Been Changed 83
If That Isn't Love 108
*In His Time 76
Into My Heart 149

*Learning to Lean 62
*Let Me Touch Him 90

*Let the Beauty of Jesus Be Seen in Me . 66
Lord, Be Glorified 113
Lord, Lay Some Soul Upon My Heart . . . 128
*Lord, We Praise You 10

*Majesty 5
My Desire 114
*My Tribute 21

Oh, How He Loves You and Me 110
Only One Life 138

Pass It On 125
*Peace in the Midst of the Storm 60

*Reach Out to Jesus 91
*Redemption Draweth Nigh 70
Right Now 148
*Rise Again 38

Seek Ye First 137
*Something Beautiful 48
*Sometimes Alleluia 8
*Spirit of the Living God 94

Ten Thousand Angels 135
The Bond of love 118
The Family of God 119
The Greatest Thing 116
*The Joy of the Lord 53
*The Longer I Serve Him 51
The Love of God 111
*The New 23rd 85
*The Trees of the Field 55
*The Wonder of It All 106
*Then I Met the Master 80
*They That Wait Upon the Lord 79
This Is the Day 99
*Thou Art Worthy 14
*Through It All 58
*'Til the Storm Passes By 32
To Be Used of God 114

*Until Then 36

*We Have Come Into His House 7
*We Must Wait 77
*We Shall Behold Him 73
*Where the Spirit of the Lord Is 97
With Eternity's Values in View 140

*Indicates songs recorded on the companion stereo cassettes
(TA-9051C) and accompaniment trax (MU-9051C, cassette).